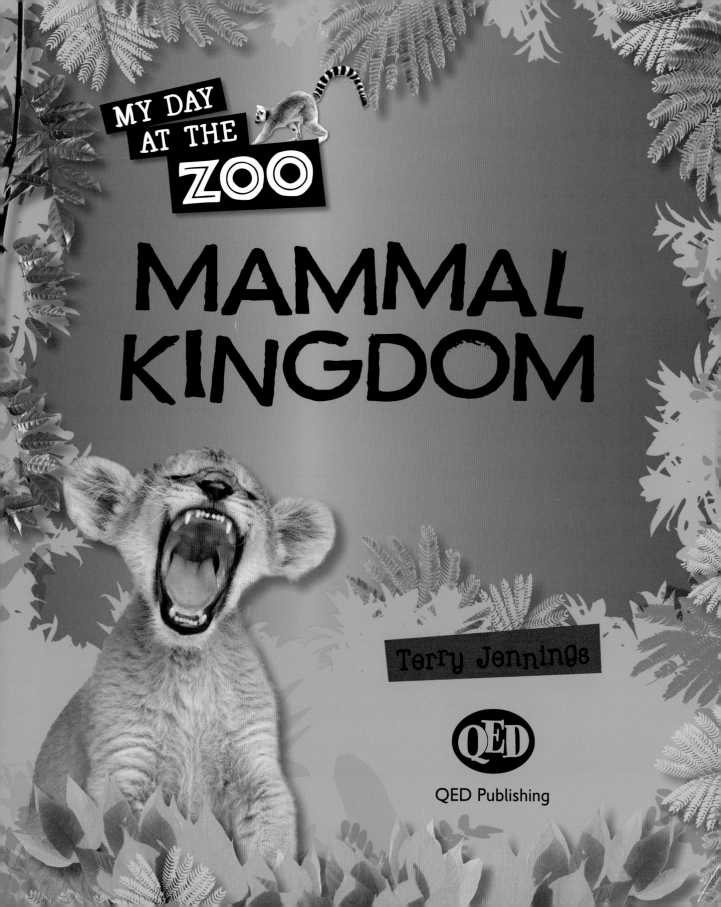

MY DAY AT THE ZOO

MAMMAL KINGDOM

Terry Jennings

QED

QED Publishing

Consultant: Steve Parker
Editor: Eve Marleau
Designer and
Picture Researcher: Liz Wiffen

First published in the UK in 2010 by
QED Publishing
A Quarto Group Company
226 City Road
London EC1V 2TT

www.qed-publishing.co.uk

ISBN 978 1 84835 394 7

Printed in China

The words in **bold** are explained in
the Glossary on page 22.

Contents

Who lives in the mammal kingdom?

Today I am going to a safari park. Animals such as lions and zebras live in zoos and safari parks. These types of animal belong to the mammal kingdom.

↑ All mammals feed their babies on milk when they are young.

A **mammal** is an animal that has hair or fur and is fed with milk from its mother's body. Many common animals, such as dogs, are mammals. Human beings are also a type of mammal.

Zoo watch

■ ELEPHANT HABITAT

ENDANGERED

The map shows where in the world the animal is from. Information about the most rare or at risk animals is given when you see the **endangered** symbol.

4

← The animals in many safari parks and zoos have lots of room to move around.

As well as letting you see lots of different animals from all over the world, safari parks and zoos also **breed** animals that are in danger of becoming **extinct**, or dying out. They work to protect the **environments** that these animals come from, too.

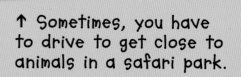

↑ Sometimes, you have to drive to get close to animals in a safari park.

Lions

At the safari park, I saw a pride of lions. They are part of the big cat family.

Male lions have a large, shaggy **mane** around their neck. Female lions are called lionesses. Their babies are called cubs.

↑ A pride of lions. The male lion is the one with the long dark hair around his head and neck.

ZOO VIEW

In the 1940s, there were about 400,000 lions in the world. Now there may be as few as 20,000. The National Geographic Society of America is helping to save the lions and other big cats from becoming extinct.

Although lions are a kind of cat, they cannot purr.
Instead, they roar to tell other lions where they are.
In Africa and India, lions hunt and kill other animals.
In safari parks, lions are fed on meat.

→ Lions yawn
when they
are tired,
just like
humans do.

■ TIGER HABITAT

Tigers

Tigers are the biggest of all cats. They are even bigger than lions. Tigers come from the forests and grasslands of Asia.

↑ A tiger's striped coat makes it very hard to spot when it is standing in long grass.

Tigers have striped coats, which helps them to be **camouflaged**, or hidden in, the grass and trees when they hunt prey. In safari parks, tigers are fed big pieces of meat, which they tear up with their long, sharp teeth.

→ Tigers can eat so much meat at one meal that sometimes they are only fed every few days.

Tigers are good swimmers. I saw a tiger make a big splash when it jumped into a pool in its **enclosure**.

→ Tigers like to cool off in water.

ZOO VIEW

In December 2008, 17 children, called the International Tiger Kids, stood by the tiger cage at the National Zoo in Washington DC, USA. They were there to ask world leaders to help stop tigers from becoming extinct.

ENDANGERED
GIRAFFES
Location: AFRICA
Population:
less than 100,000

Giraffes

Giraffes are the world's tallest animals. They come from Africa. Their long necks help them to reach leaves on the top of tall trees on which they feed.

The giraffe's spotted coat helps it to hide from lions and other animals. Some giraffes have spotty coats, while others have patches. Giraffes' coats are never exactly alike.

→ A giraffe's tongue is about 40 centimetres long.

↑ The giraffe's height helps it to spot enemies from far away.

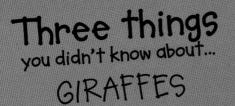

Three things
you didn't know about...
GIRAFFES

1 Although a giraffe's neck is nearly two metres long, it only has seven bones – that's the same number of bones as in your neck!

2 A giraffe's tongue is dark blue.

3 Giraffes usually stand up when they sleep. If they slept lying down, it would take them too long to get up if a **predator**, or enemy, came near.

At the safari park, I watched a giraffe drinking. Its front legs were so long that it had to spread them wide apart to get close enough to the ground to drink from a pool.

→ A giraffe has to bend down a long way to drink!

11

ZEBRA HABITAT

Zebras

Zebras come from the grasslands of Africa. They live in large groups, called herds.

A zebra's striped coat makes it hard for its enemies to see it. Zebras can run very fast – they can reach speeds of more than 65 kilometres an hour.

↓ In the wild, zebras can live for up to 25 years.

← In Africa, zebras live in large **herds** so that they can help each other watch out for danger.

In the safari park, I saw two zebras using their teeth to pick grass out of each other's fur. This is called **grooming**.

↑ Zebras groom each other's fur using their teeth.

★ ZOO STARS

In April 2004, **rangers** in a **national park** in Nairobi, Kenya, discovered a baby zebra that had no stripes — the little zebra was white all over.

Elephants

There are three kinds of elephant — the African bush and savanna elephants and the Asian elephant. They are the biggest animals on land.

trunk

tusk

large ear

African elephant

An elephant's **tusks** are two of its teeth. It uses these to scrape bark off trees and to dig up roots to eat.

An elephant's trunk is really a long nose that it uses to pick up food or suck up water. The elephant I saw sucked up water and squirted it into its mouth to drink.

→ Asian elephants have smaller ears than African elephants.

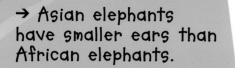

Asian elephant

small ear

← Baby elephants are called calves. They feed on their mother's milk until they are about four years old.

ZOO VIEW

In 2009, a herd of African elephants were damaging farmers' crops in Malawi. A conservation group called the International Fund for Animal Welfare, or IFAW, moved the elephants away from the crops to help the farmers.

15

Camels

Camels live in the world's hottest deserts. They have either one or two humps on their back.

humps

Bactrian camel

There are two kinds of camel – the Arabian camel and the Bactrian camel. The camels I saw were Bactrian camels, which come from Asia. They have two humps.

← A camel has wide feet to stop it from sinking in the desert sand.

16

Arabian camels

The Arabian camel has one hump. It lives in North Africa, the Middle East and India. The hump contains fat, which helps camels to survive when they cannot find food or water in the **desert**.

↑ People use Arabian camels to carry them and their goods across deserts.

Three things
you didn't know about...
CAMELS

1 Arabian camels can drink 135 litres of water in only 13 minutes.

2 Camels can run at speeds of more than 60 kilometres an hour.

3 Camels move two legs on one side of their body then two legs on the other when they run.

↑ A camel has two rows of eyelashes to protect its eyes in a sandstorm.

Kangaroos

Grey kangaroo

Kangaroos and their close relatives wallabies come from Australia. In the wild, they can live in mobs, or groups, of more than 50 kangaroos or wallabies.

When a baby kangaroo is born, it crawls up into a pouch on its mother's belly. It stays there until it is big enough to come out, which can take more than nine months. The baby kangaroo I saw was peeping out of its mother's pouch.

← This female grey kangaroo is carrying a baby in her pouch.

Kangaroos leap along on their strong back legs. They use their large tail to **balance** when they are standing up.

↑ A kangaroo stretches its tail out when it jumps to help it keep its balance.

Red kangaroo

↑ The red kangaroo is the world's largest kangaroo.

Three things
you didn't know about...
KANGAROOS

1 Young kangaroos are called joeys.

2 Kangaroos cannot move backwards.

3 When it is born, a baby kangaroo looks like a tiny pink worm. It would fit inside a teaspoon.

Monkeys

ENDANGERED
TONKIN
SNUB-NOSED
MONKEY
Location: VIETNAM
Population:
Less than 300

Most monkeys spend a lot of time in the trees, so they need to be good at climbing. Monkeys use their arms and legs to swing through the trees.

strong tail

← This spider monkey from South America uses its strong tail to hold onto branches.

The monkeys I saw were vervet monkeys. They ran down onto the cars driving around the safari park to look at the people inside.

↑ Monkeys like looking at their reflection in car windows or mirrors.

When baby monkeys are born, they are carried by their mother for about two months, until they are old enough to look after themselves.

↑ There are up to 300 kinds of monkey in the world. This is a vervet monkey from Africa.

⭐ ZOO STARS

In Brazil, brown capuchin monkeys crack open the shell of a nut using a pebble. They put the nut on a large stone, then drop the pebble onto it to crack the shell.

↑ The pygmy marmoset is the world's smallest monkey. It is about the size of an adult's hand.

Glossary

Balance To keep steady.

Breed To produce babies.

Camouflage Colours or shapes that make an animal match its surroundings.

Desert Very dry land where few plants can grow.

Enclosure An area with a fence or wall around it.

Extinct Not existing anymore; when every one of a kind of animal or plant has died out.

Endangered Describes an animal or plant that is in danger of becoming extinct.

Environment The surroundings of an animal or another living thing.

Grooming To clean one's hair or fur.

Herd A number of zebras, cows or other animals living together.

Mammal An animal that feeds on its mother's milk when it is young.

Mane The long hair on the back and neck of a lion, horse or other animal.

National park A large area of land where animals and plants are protected.

Predator An animal that catches and eats other animals.

Ranger Someone who looks after a park or forest.

Tusk One of the two very long pointed teeth of an elephant. Other animals, such as walruses, boars and narwhals, also have tusks.

Index

Notes for parents and teachers

- Discuss with children why it is necessary to be quiet and not run when visiting a safari park. Explain why they need to wash their hands carefully after touching an animal or any part of its enclosure, and particularly before touching food.

- Look through the book together. How many of the animals in the book can children recognize?

- All of the animals described in this book are mammals. Across the world, there are about 5400 species of wild mammal. How many more kinds of mammals do children know? Point out that most mammals do not lay eggs, but instead their eggs grow into babies inside the mother's body.

- Discuss with your child what is meant by extinction and why some animals are in danger of becoming extinct. The main causes of extinction are hunting, the effects of pollution and the destruction of the animals' natural habitat. If safari parks and zoos are able to breed endangered animals, they will not be able to release these animals into the wild unless a safe place can be found for them.

- Explore movement and ask children to move like a lion, a kangaroo or a monkey.

- Introduce children to the word 'camouflage'. Look at the book together. Which of the animals are camouflaged? Which other animals can children think of that use camouflage?

- Do the children have a favourite mammal? Why is this animal their favourite?

- Some useful websites for more information:
  www.bbc.co.uk/nature/animals/mammals
  www.sandiegozoo.org
  www.kids.yahoo.com/animals/mammals
  www.zsl.org/education/
  www.nwf.org/wildlife
  www.thebigzoo.com
  www.arkive.org
  www.uksafari.com
  www.defenders.org/wildlife__and__habitat

Website information is correct at time of going to press. However, the publishers cannot accept liability for any information or links found on third-party websites.